Life In The Pond

Written by Eileen Curran

Illustrated by Elizabeth Ellis

Troll Associates

Library of Congress Cataloging in Publication Data

Curran, Eileen.
    Life in the pond.

    Summary: Looks at the frogs, fish, beavers, birds,
and other animals living in or near a pond.
    1. Pond fauna—Juvenile literature. [1. Pond animals]
I. Ellis, Elizabeth, ill.   II. Title.
QL146.3.C87   1985   591.52'6322   84-16285
ISBN 0-8167-0452-X (lib. bdg.)
ISBN 0-8167-0453-8 (pbk.)

Chirp, buzz, splash!

The sun is rising. It is a new day.

The pond is a busy place. Can you see the animals?
What a wonderful place it can be.

Hop. The frog jumps.
Chirp. The birds sing.

Splash. The fish swim.
What a busy place the pond is!

Can you see the animals?

The sun is shining.
It is a warm day.

Buzz. The bees fly.

Splash. The beavers swim.

Quack. The ducks play.
What a busy place the pond is!

Can you see the animals?
Who lives near the pond?

Now the sun is setting.

It is night. *Whoosh*. The wind blows.

Chirp. The crickets sing.
Who-o-o. The owl calls.

What a busy place the pond is!

What a wonderful place it can be.